TABLE OF CONTENTS

INTRODUCTION

The information contained in this handbook can be utilized by organizations, as well as individuals seeking a higher level of personal or professional "success."

Throughout this handbook, we will be following an eight-step "success map," which was developed from research showing that the process of achieving success is remarkably consistent from person to person and organization to organization. These eight steps will provide you with the means for achieving success and securing goals on a day-to-day basis.

Here is what the eight-step method will do for you:

- Help you identify the values which dictate your goals
- Provide a framework for achieving those goals

The eight-step method includes:

1. Examining your identity
2. Defining your values
3. Establishing goals
4. Putting together an action plan
5. Examining various facets of motivation
6. Establishing discipline
7. Maintaining flexibility
8. Reaching an outcome

The "success map" for individuals, families, departments or organizations is as follows:

Identity → Values → Goals → Action Plan
↓
Motivation → Discipline
↓
Flexibility → Outcome

However, having a model, in and of itself, will not guarantee success. One must have the motivation and persistence to follow the model. In the words of Calvin Coolidge, "*Nothing in the world can take the place of persistence. Talent will not; nothing is more common than unsuccessful men with talent. Genius will not; unrewarded genius is almost a proverb. Education will not; the world is full of educated derelicts. Persistence and determination are omnipotent. The slogan 'press on' has solved and always will solve the problems of the human race.*"

This handbook will show you how each of the eight steps can lead you down the road to success in your personal and professional life.

After reading this chapter, you will be able to:

List the eight steps of the success map;

Explain the relevance of identity and values to goal-setting; and

Begin to examine your own personal and professional life by completing the "What's Important to Me" worksheet.

1 THE EIGHT-STEP SUCCESS MODEL: AN OVERVIEW

In this chapter, you will be introduced to the eight-step "success map" we will follow throughout the book. An overview of the entire model will be included, with a subsequent chapter devoted to each of the eight success map components.

In order to understand where you want to go on your journey to achieving success, you must first identify your desired outcome. As Stephen Covey, author of the best-seller *The 7 Habits of Highly Effective People* writes, the second habit of successful people is to "begin with the end in mind." Simply stated, this means to start with a clear understanding of your ultimate destination so that your actions each and every day will bring you closer to your destination.

Outcome

Do not confuse goals with outcomes. Goals are conceptual; they represent the ideal state which you aspire to — the one which guides all your actions. Outcome is what actually happens, which may or may not be what you originally targeted on your success map. In some instances, the actual outcome may be more desirable than your original goal. That's where your ability to adapt and remain flexible over time will be a valuable attribute.

Achieving a desired outcome may involve earning a college degree, receiving a sought-after promotion, buying your first home or mastering a new sport. Whatever the end, the process for a successful outcome is the same — setting a goal which is consistent with your true identity and sustaining the necessary motivation over time.

Identity

Identity ⟶ Importance

The importance of analyzing your true identity prior to setting a goal cannot be underestimated. A lack of identity often results in a lack of direction in goal-setting. Failure to analyze your true identity causes confusion and results in goal-setting which is inconsistent with who or what you would like to become. Therefore, the key question is: Who am I?

Your answer should be an accurate assessment that examines how you see yourself, how others see you, how you choose to spend your time, the quality of your relationships and your strengths, skills and weaknesses. You cannot force yourself to perform in a way that is not in alignment with how you perceive yourself. If you do, no matter how successful you are in achieving others' standards, you will feel that you have failed.

Next, take a moment to ask yourself, "What is my identity within the organization? Am I perceived as a leader? A manager? Is this how I wish to be perceived? Do my professional-related expectations mesh with the expectations of the company (or department) I work for? Can this organization provide me with opportunities that are in alignment with my personal and professional identity?"

Oftentimes, you can get so busy working that you may no longer understand or relish the role you play in the organization.

On the following page is a "Professional Identity Assessment" worksheet. Completion of this worksheet will assist you in determining your current identity on the job — both from your perspective and from that of those who work with you. With nearly 50 percent of your day spent at work, it is important that your work be in alignment with your personal and professional identity. For example, if you see yourself as a nurturing, empathic person, a job which requires you to work exclusively with machines would not be personally satisfying in the long run.

Success Map

Directions: Circle the appropriate answer to the questions below.

1.	Are you challenged by life?	Yes	No	Sometimes
2.	Do you take action when problems arise?	Yes	No	Sometimes
3.	Do you set goals for your financial future?	Yes	No	Sometimes
4.	Do you set goals for career achievements?	Yes	No	Sometimes
5.	Do you have enough energy for your work/personal endeavors?	Yes	No	Sometimes
6.	Do you have a sense of humor?	Yes	No	Sometimes
7.	Are you a good friend?	Yes	No	Sometimes
8.	Do you like yourself?	Yes	No	Sometimes
9.	Are you a good listener?	Yes	No	Sometimes
10.	Are you a mentor?	Yes	No	Sometimes
11.	Are you a team player?	Yes	No	Sometimes
12.	Do you enjoy your work?	Yes	No	Sometimes
13.	Are you time-conscious?	Yes	No	Sometimes
14.	Do you have good instincts?	Yes	No	Sometimes
15.	Do your co-workers like you?	Yes	No	Sometimes

These questions are designed to help you think about your identity — what you like about yourself as well as adjustments you may want to make. The answers may provide you with valuable insights when beginning the goal-setting process.

A clear sense of personal and professional identity results in effective goal-setting. Whether you are trying to increase your own personal motivation or that of co-workers, remember these three important steps:

1. Break down goals into smaller "sub-goals" that can be successfully completed, leading to continual positive outcomes.

2. Reward yourself and others for successes on the way to the ultimate goal's completion.

3. Minimize the opportunity for failure by providing adequate information or training on the task to be completed. This may mean reading an instruction manual, attending a class or receiving one-on-one training.

Strive to reach these goals because they give meaning to who you are and what you believe in.

The same concepts apply to job-related motivation of yourself and others. If the organizational goals represent the ideologies and values of the employee, motivation to achieve those goals is greatly increased because the worker will identify with and support the desired outcome. For example, if one of your personal goals is helping and healing others, any organizational goals which benefit nonprofit health care will be in alignment with your personal goal.

Another factor leading to a high level of motivation to achieve a goal is the level of involvement the person had in setting the goal. For example, when organizations tell employees at the beginning of each year what goals the company has set, they reduce the likelihood of achieving those goals. Why? Because the employees do not feel personally committed to the goals — goals which were defined by "someone" else. Successful employee-centered organizations allow workers to have input in the goal-setting process, thus increasing the workers' commitment to goal achievement.

As a manager and motivator of others, for several reasons it is your responsibility to involve your staff in setting job-related goals. First, it ensures that the goals are realistic yet challenging; second, it demonstrates your appreciation of their job-related knowledge and competency; third, it instills commitment to attaining the goal — which serves to continually motivate and inspire.

So far, you have learned what motivation is, how negative and positive consequences impact the degree of motivation and the positive impact appropriate goal-setting plays in the motivation of self and others.

What, then, can be done when the desire and excitement begin to wane? How can you re-instill a sense of commitment and energy to goal achievement?

One methodology used by athletes, teachers and sales managers is the visual charting of one's progress. Athletes keep detailed logs of daily schedules, "wins and losses" and physiological changes. Educators post grades, and sales managers post daily sales and percentage of goal figures. When positive progress is visually represented, the brain receives subliminal messages which encourage and reinforce. When less-than-desired progress is charted, deviations are clearly identified before irreparable consequences occur.

Another effective method of motivating yourself and others is the appropriate use of praise and recognition — "appropriate" being the operative word. Many people believe they are effective motivators because they dole out praise and recognition in abundance. Quality, not quantity, is the key.

Values

Values are the ideas or beliefs which guide your actions on a daily basis. The more you are true to your values, the more your personal and professional lives will be "in sync." For example, if you believe in or value honesty, you will act in ways which are honest and seek the company of other honest people.

In Your Personal Life

Your personal values govern your behavior toward other people, the types of relationships you seek, your attitude toward what is right and wrong and your fundamental convictions.

In Your Professional Life

Think about the "culture" that exists where you work.

- Are the ethics in harmony with yours?
- Are you proud of your company and co-workers or employees?
- Does your job or role as small business owner make you feel good?

Your work should support your personal and professional values. If it does not, then you must seek other opportunities which do. Values are developed early on in your life and do not change drastically over time. Therefore, to expect your values to change to match those of your co-workers or supervisors is not likely. There are many reasons why identity and values may be different. The greater the gap between them, the more likely you are to be unhappy or to underperform in your career.

Goals

You can create an outcome that is empty if your goals aren't relevant to your personal life, your career, your business or your job expectations. Worthy goals are based on values that are well thought out and honest.

It's estimated that less than five percent of the population has clearly defined goals. Without them, you can't possibly progress down the road.

In Your Personal Life

Your mind contains a homing device similar to one in a guided missile. If you start to go off course, your goals will point you once again in the right direction.

In Your Professional Life

At work, you have to be aware of not only your career goals but also those of the company and of your supervisor. If you're a small business owner, you will determine your own goals as well as those of your company, but you also should take the goals of your employees into consideration.

Enlightened companies share their plans and business objectives with employees. As a small business owner, this practice should be high on your list of priorities. If you work for a company that routinely shares this information with employees, then you can set your goals so they are consistent with those of your organization. If your goals are not in alignment with your organization's goals, you should seriously consider a different job. Setting goals is your third step.

Action Plan

Identity → Values → Goals → **Action Plan** → Outcome

Action plans are based on the information gleaned from defining your identity, values and goals, coupled with the effort you are willing to make to realize your intended outcome. You also need to look at your resources. You don't want to define an action plan that you are unable to implement because of inadequate time, energy or money.

In Your Personal Life

Develop your personal action plan. List the steps you need to take and the resources required to accomplish these goals. Prioritize the steps. Now you know what is required to accomplish each of your goals.

In Your Professional Life

An action plan is a statement of the logical, step-by-step flow of actions you need to take to effect results.

Factors to consider when creating an action plan.

- What needs to be done?
- Who should do it?
- When is the deadline?
- How will it be done?

Motivation

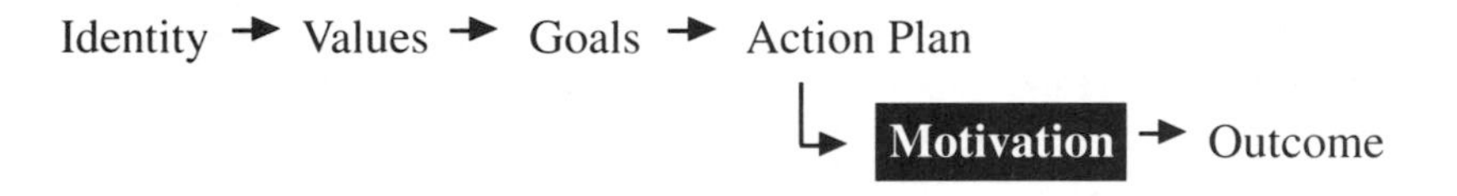

No one ever does anything without having been motivated to do it. Every thought you think, every act in which you voluntarily engage can be traced back to some definite motive or combination of motives.

Motivation is by far the step that has generated the most debate, study and theories. This book takes a practical approach by boiling motivation down to this: If you are rewarded or recognized for doing something, you will be motivated; if you reward others, they will be motivated.

We'll look at various aspects of this extraordinarily complex area:

- A definition
- Acceptance of people
- Forms of reward
- Praise and criticism
- Involvement
- Keeping score
- Self-motivation

In Your Personal Life

Motivation is the result of desire. It is the desire to get out of bed each morning, to take the next step in your action plan, to overcome adversity and be successful. It is the desire to do what is necessary to realize your goals. Motivation is also what drives you to be excellent day after day.

In Your Professional Life

Often the key question is: How do you motivate people? If you can show another person how he or she is going to benefit from doing something, you have a motivated employee or co-worker. Motivation is your fifth step.

Discipline

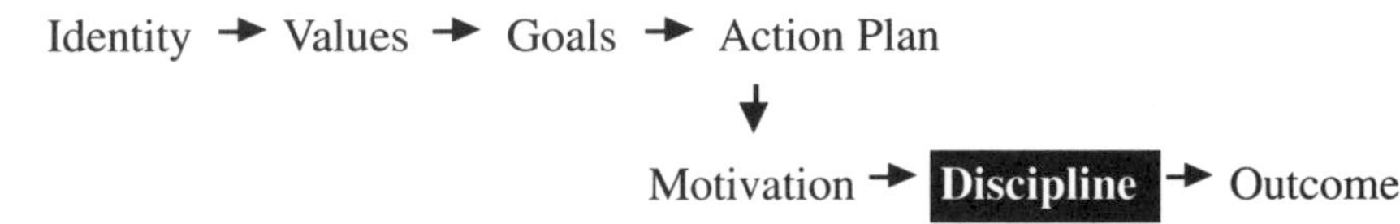

Successful people don't succumb to procrastination or temporary setbacks. They call upon an inner strength to overcome obstacles.

In Your Personal Life

Discipline in your personal life may be the hardest step to take. Whether it involves dieting, exercising or controlling your temper, it's not fun. But it can be learned and developed, and the more you use it, the more you will have control over your life.

In Your Professional Life

The discipline you must adhere to on the job is often not self-imposed. Discipline on the job functions best when it starts at the top — when the standards are clear, fair, understood and actually used. Discipline is step six on your map.

Flexibility

Identity → Values → Goals → Action Plan
↓
Motivation → Discipline
↓
Flexibility → Outcome

You must be able to modify your strategies and adapt your action plan when changes occur. This will require continual re-evaluation on your part.

In Your Personal Life

Your personal values evolve as you mature, as your priorities shift and as your family situation changes. By constantly re-evaluating yourself, your values, goals and action plan, you can adapt to change.

In Your Professional Life

There are dozens of variables that can change on the job: a change in pay structure or work hours, a new supervisor or new ownership of the company. Successful people know that one key to success is flexibility — step seven on our journey.

The chapters in this handbook follow the eight-step road map, starting with understanding your true *identity* (Step 1) to arriving at an *outcome (Step 8)*. If you travel through all eight steps, you will almost surely gain more achievements and satisfaction than you had before.

Success Map

Directions: Answer the following questions. Your answers will assist you in setting meaningful goals which are relevant to your identity and values.

1. What is the last thing you learned about yourself?

   ____

   ____

2. What was your latest raise or promotion at work? ______________
3. When was the last time you discussed an exciting idea not related to your job? ______________________________
4. Do you have written long-term goals for your career?___________
5. Name the last spontaneous "fun" thing you did.

   ____

6. Who is your mentor? ______________________________
7. Do you have written long-term financial goals? ______________
8. What two goals would you like to achieve this year?

   ____

   ____

9. Name two people you find interesting and would like to know better.

   ____

   ____

10. What three things would you like your children to inherit from you as a person?

    ____

    ____

    ____

After reading this chapter, you will gain perspective on self-identity by:

- ✔ Completing the three self-inventory exercises;
- ✔ Avoiding defining yourself in terms of "things," "shoulds" and "stereotypical roles"; and
- ✔ Reflecting on the six case study questions.

2 IDENTITY: BECOMING AWARE OF WHO YOU ARE

Identity ⟶ Importance

Defining your identity will keep you focused as you set priorities, organize tasks, deal with emergencies and accomplish challenges in your personal and business lives. If you have no concept of your identity, you run the risk of trying to be everything and do everything in a random, haphazard way.

Defining Your Personal Identity

The first step in defining your identity involves self-awareness — understanding who you currently are, as well as who you want to become. Taking inventory of yourself can be an uncomfortable and even painful experience, but it is necessary if you want to improve.

Knowing yourself well should be seen as an extremely important process leading to your ultimate happiness and success in both your personal and professional lives.

The self-inventory should include an evaluation of:

- Your attitudes
- Your self-image
- How you treat other people

As you reflect on these aspects of your life, avoid:

1. ***Defining yourself in terms of external "things."*** It's easy to define yourself by external trappings: cars, clothes, job titles, your business success, etc. But what happens to your identity if you lose the expensive car and the powerful job title or even your business?

   Focus on the things in your life that endure: the personal relationships that are important to you, the quality of your life, your professional ethics and goals, your personal integrity.

2. ***Defining yourself in terms of "shoulds."*** When you make decisions or behave because you feel you "should," you might be letting others' expectations determine your identity. (Obviously, some "shoulds" are the result of commitments you have made or adherence to laws and social conventions and *should* be honored.) Separate others' expectations from what *you* expect of yourself.

3. ***Defining yourself in terms of stereotypical "roles."*** Traditional, stereotypical roles such as "wife/mother/nurturer," "husband/father/provider," "career woman," "corporate executive" and "business owner" can limit your potential.

Success Map

Directions: Before you begin the journey, take some time to identify who you are.

When I think about myself, I'm proud of:

____

____

____

____

My best friend describes me as (qualities, skills, characteristics)

____

____

____

____

The three most important areas of my personal life are:

1. ______________________________________
2. ______________________________________
3. ______________________________________

Defining Your Professional Identity

If you are like many people, you take your job so seriously that your identity becomes closely associated with what you do and where you work or the business you own. Here are some questions to ask yourself:

- How do I spend my time on the job? (Different from a job description.)
- What are my people strengths?
- What are my major problem areas?
- Are my skills being fully utilized?
- Do I like the way I'm treated on the job?

If you are a supervisor and trying to determine your department's identity, you might want to discuss how your group contributes to the larger corporate identity and purpose. A group meeting is an excellent forum to discuss these questions. As a business owner, you also can conduct sessions with employees to discuss your company's identity and purpose. You want the advantage of hearing from as many people as possible.

Positive change results when you know your professional identity. For instance, you can drop activities that cause you to stray from your original mission.

Success Map

The three most important job functions I currently perform are:

1. ____
2. ____
3. ____

My description of an "ideal" job or career is:

____

____

____

____

My current job allows me to express my "true" identity ___yes ___ no

The way in which my co-workers view me is consistent with how I view myself ___yes ___ no

If I could, I would re-structure my job in the following ways:

____

____

____

Case Study:

Throughout the remainder of this handbook, we follow Margo, a 27-year-old computer programmer, as she uses the eight-step "success map" to set and achieve her personal and professional goals. Margo is currently divorced, living in a small, one-bedroom apartment.

Prior to setting her goals, Margo must first determine her identity. To do so she asks herself a number of questions.

1. ***How do I feel about myself?*** Margo generally has a healthy degree of self-esteem. She projects a bright, optimistic attitude about life.

2. ***How do people treat me, both on and off the job?*** In her personal life, Margo has many friends. She meets people very easily, and they respond to her quickly.

   She gets respect off the job, but it's a different story where she works. Her last performance review was not good. Her boss said she has a bad attitude.

   By considering this question, it allowed her to see clearly, for the first time, the difference in the way she's treated when she's working as opposed to when she's not.

3. ***How do I spend my time on the job?*** She works at a computer terminal all day long. She has very little contact with other people. At first she found her job stimulating; now she's so bored she can't wait to leave work in the evening, and she dreads going to work every morning.

4. ***What do I do when I'm not working?*** In her spare time, Margo often participates in animal-rights demonstrations. This is very much unlike her colleagues, many of whom spend their leisure time tinkering with their own personal computers. This often makes her feel like an outcast.

5. ***What are my strengths?*** Margo knows she is a "people-person." She's a very caring person, which explains her desire to work with animals. She's also conscientious. Although she is no longer excited about her job, she still takes pride in her performance.

6. ***What are my weaknesses?*** Margo has difficulty managing her finances. She usually is a month behind in paying her bills. She's not careful about her physical appearance. She is not ambitious and blames that for not having a game plan to change her situation.

Margo is doing what every person and organization must do periodically. She is becoming aware of her own identity, which is step one on the road map.

Identity ——→ Importance

You will follow Margo as she progresses along the eight-step path toward a better life and higher achievement.

When you become aware of your identity, you might not like what you see. One reason is that your behavior may not be consistent with your values, which is the subject of the next chapter.

Success Map

Directions: Get a quick snapshot of who you are before moving on to Chapter 3.

1.	Are you happy?	Yes	No
2.	Do you spend time with your friends?	Yes	No
3.	Do you exercise at least three times a week?	Yes	No
4.	Do you play a sport, a musical instrument, paint or take classes for interest only?	Yes	No
5.	Are you challenged by your job?	Yes	No
6.	Do you feel good about your future?	Yes	No
7.	Have you read a book for enjoyment this month?	Yes	No
8.	Do you like who you are?	Yes	No
9.	Do you take "real" vacations?	Yes	No
10.	Do you have a mentor?	Yes	No
11.	Do you take a lunch "break" at least four times a week?	Yes	No
12.	Are you a "strong" person?	Yes	No
13.	Can you make and feel confident with your decisions?	Yes	No
14.	Are you good at your job skills?	Yes	No
15.	Do you trust your instincts?	Yes	No

Do your responses reflect the type of person you want to be? For those statements to which you answered "no," are you satisfied with your response? In subsequent chapters we will discuss goal-setting and action planning strategies which will turn your "nos" to "yeses."

After reading this chapter, you will be able to:

 Explain why values are important personally and professionally; and

☑ List your top five most important values.

3 HOW TO DETERMINE YOUR VALUES

Identity → **Values** ——————→ Outcome

How would you like to dream for months about going on a great vacation full of hurried sight-seeing and museum tours, only to realize at the trip's end that you *really* wanted to lie on a quiet beach? The same thing can happen if the objectives in your life are not based on sound values.

What are values? They are your most important fundamental beliefs. Values provide you with structure that helps you organize your life.

If you clarify your values, you create a basic structure upon which you can build your personal life, your career, your business and all other important aspects of your life. Values go by different names:

- Principles
- Purpose
- Convictions
- Ideals
- Beliefs

You must understand your values before you can formulate meaningful goals and your action plan.

Your Personal Values

Here are some questions that will help you determine your personal values:

- What is my attitude toward other people?
- What three moral issues are important to me?
- What are my obligations to community, country and family?
- What ideals or core beliefs do I want to instill in my children?

Your answers will help you identify your fundamental values and how they affect your personal relationships. You must look inside yourself and determine what is important to you. You should do it frequently. Defining your values gives you the energy and focus to pursue your goals.

Professional Values

If an organization or business instills sound values and insists that those values be a part of daily life from top management on down, it can be a tremendous motivating force and bring people together as part of a team working for a common purpose.

Success Map

Directions: Review the following list several times, place a check mark by those values that are important to you. Next, prioritize those that are most important by numbering them 1 through 10, 1 being most important.

Security
Wealth
Good Health
Relationship with Spouse/Mate
Relationship with Children
Relationship with Family (Parents/ other Relatives)
Fame
Job/Career
Power
Happiness
Friendship
Retirement
Being in Business for Yourself
Long Life
Travel
Respect of Peers
Power
Spiritual Fulfillment
Charity/Contributing to Others (Money or Time)
__________ Other

Look carefully at the top five most important values. Do you need to make any adjustments to what you "thought" you wanted? Eighty percent of your energy should be devoted to those five values. Write them below and post them where you will see them every day to keep you focused on what is most important. It will drive your actions!

Cut out and put in an important place.

The following beliefs, principles and values are the foundation to my success:

1. ______________________________
2. ______________________________
3. ______________________________
4. ______________________________
5. ______________________________

Case Study:

Margo has committed the time and energy to work on her values. In defining her values, she concentrated on four key areas.

- Her relationships with others
- Her work environment
- Her contribution to society
- Her personal fulfillment

To determine her values in each of these four areas, she asked herself the following questions.

1. ***How important is having contact with people, especially on the job?*** She determined that relationships with friends and co-workers are more important to her than they are for most people. She finds this ironic, because as a computer programmer she has very little interaction with people. Many of her colleagues distrust others and the unpredictable way people often behave.

2. ***What do I value most in a work environment?*** Margo has a good friend who genuinely loves her job. She said that on her birthday she received a card with a warm, handwritten message from her boss. Margo determined that her friend's work environment is very much like Margo's own personality — warm and friendly — and that she would fit very nicely into a similar work environment.

3. ***Do I feel a need to make the world a better place?*** Yes. Margo has a strong need to help others, especially those who can't help themselves. For her, this means animals. She feels very little of this need is being satisfied in her current situation.

4. ***What are my priorities in terms of personal fulfillment?*** Money is not as important to Margo as other things. She places great emphasis on experiencing joy and having a positive attitude about life, which she affirms frequently at her church. Friendships also matter a great deal to her. Her appearance and health are of secondary importance to her at this time.

As a result, Margo concludes that her values are:

- Cultivating and maintaining strong personal relationships with friends, family members and co-workers.
- A preference for a warm, emotionally supportive work environment. She might be willing to take a lower salary to achieve this.
- Committing her time and energy to help animals.
- To be surrounded by positive people and influences.

Determining values is the second step on your road map to success.

Identity → **Values** ——————→ Outcome

Establishing values allows you to set goals in order of priority. Without values, all goals are equally important. Goal-setting is the subject of the next chapter.

After reading this chapter, you will be able to:

- Name three reasons why most people fail to set goals;

- List six principles for goal setting; and
- Set five goals for your personal life and five for your professional career.

4 DEFINING YOUR GOALS

If you've ever tried to plow a field, you know this to be true: If you don't look at a fixed point on the horizon, your rows will meander all over the field.

The same is true in your life. Without keeping sight of a specific goal, you are likely to wander off course. Yet less than five percent of the population sets goals. Why?

1. ***It's hard work.*** It requires time and soul-searching.
2. ***Fear of failure.*** If you don't set goals, you can't fail. True. But you can't succeed either.
3. ***Fear of success.*** Some people don't value themselves enough to feel they deserve success.

If you find yourself saying, "I don't have enough time" or "I don't have the education," understand that these are all excuses. If you aren't successful, did you plan to fail? Most people do not set goals because they are not sure what they want, they don't know how to set goals, they are afraid they won't reach them or they have poor self-esteem. To reach a goal, you must be able to see where you want to go, and then, when you arrive, you'll see even farther. You have the potential to be whatever you want to be, but you first have to decide what that is. What follows are guidelines for setting effective goals.

In Your Personal Life

1. ***Goals should be an extension of your values.*** When goals support what you believe in, life becomes meaningful and exciting. Goals based on values make it easier for you to determine your priorities. Prioritize goals, and then focus your efforts on no more than 2-3 of your highest priorities. Research has shown that people are most effective when they limit their activities to a maximum of three simultaneous goals.

2. ***Goals should be specific.*** Goals such as happiness, success and wealth are too vague to be effective. Here are some examples of specific goals:

    - To have a net worth of $200,000 by the time I'm 40 years old

    - To graduate from college by next May

    - To lose 25 pounds by the end of the year

    Each of the above goals has a defined objective and deadline that allows you to measure your progress.

3. ***Goals should be written.*** Writing down your goals represents a commitment and has been proven to have a powerful influence on the brain's subconscious.

4. ***Set challenging but realistic goals.*** Be realistic. Don't pledge to be president of your company by the end of the year if you are now a file clerk. Set intermediate short-term goals which bring you closer to your ultimate goals.

    When you dream big, be careful with whom you share your goals. Many people laugh at dreamers, so keep your goals to yourself or share them only with supportive people.

5. ***Visualize your goals.*** The more details your visualized goals contain, the easier it is for the subconscious to embrace them. When your mind accepts your visualized goal as reality, you will work long and hard to achieve it.

6. ***Reward yourself.*** This provides incentive and helps overcome roadblocks such as procrastination. Figure out ahead of time how you'll reward yourself after you accomplish your goal:

    - Promise yourself dinner at your favorite restaurant.

    - Plan a vacation after you earn your MBA.

    - Throw a big party after remodeling your house.

Success Map

Directions: Referring to the values you identified in chapter 3, record five of your most important personal values.

1. ______________________________
2. ______________________________
3. ______________________________
4. ______________________________
5. ______________________________

Think about these five values, and list below five goals for your personal life. Remember, goals should:

- Be specific
- Be measurable, if possible
- Be realistic
- Be visualized

1. ______________________________
2. ______________________________
3. ______________________________
4. ______________________________
5. ______________________________

In Your Professional Life

The same goal-setting guidelines that work in your personal life also apply to your career.

1. ***Base your career goals on values.*** If an organization has a clearly articulated statement of philosophy and values, there can be a meshing of corporate and personal goals known as alignment.

   If you are a supervisor or business owner, allow your staff members to shape group values. As a result, your goals, the goals of other people and the organization's goals take on a new dimension. They are motivating because they are integrated.

2. ***Set specific goals.*** Examples of goals that are too vague:

   - Increase productivity
   - Decrease turnover

   The same goals could be stated:

   - Increase the business's average daily quota 15 percent by the end of the fiscal year
   - Decrease turnover by March to less than 10 percent annually from the current rate of 28 percent

   Each of these goals is measurable and has a deadline, which is characteristic of specific goals.

3. ***Write down professional goals.*** Write out goals in one memorable, concise statement.

4. ***Set attainable goals.*** Dream big but be realistic. Goals that are out of reach only cause frustration.

5. ***Visualize goals.*** If you are a supervisor or business owner, share your vision, and the goals will become a powerful motivational tool.

6. ***Establish rewards.*** Let people know in advance that they will receive some kind of reward when a goal is realized. It doesn't have to be money. It can be:

    - A party
    - A day of training to further people's careers
    - A day off
    - A special privilege like a reserved parking space

Success Map

Directions: Look back at your list of ten most important values and choose five regarding your professional career.

1. ______________________________
2. ______________________________
3. ______________________________
4. ______________________________
5. ______________________________

Think about these five values, and list below five goals for your professional career.

1. ______________________________
2. ______________________________
3. ______________________________
4. ______________________________
5. ______________________________

Remember, goals should:

- Be specific
- Be measurable, if possible
- Be realistic
- Be visualized

Case Study:

It's now time for Margo to engage in goal-setting. She likes people and animals, and she has contact with neither in her current job. She has investigated occupations where she could work with animals, but in most cases the salaries are too low.

Margo would have to go to school for six months to get certified as a veterinary technician, but she could keep her current job in the meantime. Her peer group would then be other people who share her love of animals. She visualizes herself in a white coat, helping save an animal's life, then seeing the smile and gratitude of a happy pet owner.

A veterinary technician earns less than she currently does. However, within two years, she plans on becoming the head technician, which would put her just about at her current salary level.

Margo's goals are:

- To be a veterinary technician in six months
- To pay all bills within 90 days
- To save $1000 in the next year
- To make at least one good new friend each month

Thinking about goals is necessary for success. But thinking is not doing. How to put your goals into action is discussed in the next chapter.

After reading this chapter, you will be able to:

 Name steps you can take to make your goals a reality;

 Develop action plans to reach your goals; and

Commit to record and review your progress on a routine basis.

5 WRITING YOUR ACTION PLAN

Identity → Values → Goals → **Action Plan** → Outcome

An action plan answers this question: "How" will I achieve the "What" (goal)? It's the specific steps needed to accomplish the result we want. Where do you start? What strategies will work best? What resources will give you the outcome you want?

There are definite steps you can take to make goals reality.

In Your Personal Life

1. ***Create a goal activity page.*** You should have one sheet of paper for each of your goals. At the top of the first page, write your highest-priority goal. State it concisely and in specific language. On the left side of the page, list all the activities that will enable you to reach that goal in order of importance. In a column to the right of each step, list who or what can help you accomplish that step. In a third column, write a target date for accomplishing each activity. Use this approach for your top three to five goals.

2. ***Start now.*** NOW is the secret word of success. The best place to start is with the first activity that corresponds with your most important goal. Focus on it, then do the following:

   - Spend a minimum of five minutes each day doing a step(s) under your top goal.

- Don't wait until conditions are perfect. Expect problems. Tackle each one as soon as you encounter it.

- If you fear taking action, focus just on what is required to complete a single activity.

3. ***Record your progress.*** Charting your daily efforts and subsequent progress provides you with the motivation needed to achieve your ultimate goal. This can be done via a daily journal, a progress chart or entries into a calendar or time management organizer. Health clubs and weight loss centers have recognized the positive impact of frequently charting daily results. Progress in the desired direction provides the perseverance needed to carry on. Progress away from your goal can easily and quickly be deleted and corrected before a more permanent outcome is realized.

In Your Professional Life

Nothing will put you in control better than having an action plan for accomplishing your professional and departmental or business goals.

Yet most of us don't spend enough time planning. Often it's because:

- Putting out today's fires is often more critical than thinking about tomorrow. Ironically, putting out fires means you are not focusing on what's important: taking steps to avoid future problems.

- It's easy to believe that planning should be done at the highest levels of an organization. Not true. It's something that should be done with your organizational group no matter the level or size.

- Planning takes a commitment of time and energy. But if you don't plan, you'll find yourself wasting time and energy doing the things that could have been avoided.

For Your Job, Departmental or Business Action Plan

1. ***Write it down.*** You may need to use a planning sheet that's more detailed than the one in this book, but the format should be the same. For each goal, list all activities necessary to accomplish it; then list who or what it will take to get them done. Then decide on a time frame.

2. ***Begin now.*** Develop your action plans immediately and review and use them on a daily basis. This builds confidence in leadership, and consequently, the people you work with or those who work for you will be more motivated. By saying "yes" to a project or course of action, you are also saying "no" to something else less important. Action plans make the best use of your time by telling you what needs to be done right now.

Case Study:

Margo's most important goal is to change careers. Her goal at the top of her activity page reads: to become a veterinary technician within six months.

Here is a list of her activities:

- Get literature on schools that offer courses in becoming a veterinary technician. Deadline — two weeks
- Apply for admission. Deadline — one month
- Apply for financial assistance. Deadline — one month
- Start school at night. Deadline — two months
- Graduate. Deadline — eight months
- Search for job and get a job. Deadline — 10 months
- Earn first paycheck as a veterinary technician. Deadline — 12 months

Margo has taken the fourth step on her road map to success:

Identity → Values → Goals → **Action Plan** → Outcome

Complete the Success Map and Action Planning Activities on the following pages.

Success Map

Identify what you want to achieve this year and in three years and prioritize the top three targets.

This Year: ____________________ Three Years:____________________

Personal

_____ ____________________

_____ ____________________

_____ ____________________

Professional

_____ ____________________

_____ ____________________

_____ ____________________

Personal

_____ ____________________

_____ ____________________

_____ ____________________

Professional

_____ ____________________

_____ ____________________

_____ ____________________

Select your top "whats" and convert to a goal using the following:

Personal

To ________ ______________ by ______________ by ______________.

verb subject standard (i.e., %) date/deadline

Professional

To ________ ______________ by ___________ by __________________.

verb subject standard (i.e., %) date/deadline

Success Map continued...

Next, think step-by-step of "how" you'll achieve your goal; record your progress on a routine basis.

Personal Goal #1		Action Plan	Who	When	Status
________	1.	________			
________	2.	________			
________	3.	________			
________	4.	________			
________	5.	________			

Professional Goal #1		Action Plan	Who	When	Status
________	1.	________			
________	2.	________			
________	3.	________			
________	4.	________			
________	5.	________			

After reading this chapter, you will be able to:

 Describe the importance of positive consequences to motivation;

 List the five basic needs that motivate people; and

Explain why negative motivation is often ineffective.

6 MOTIVATING YOURSELF AND OTHERS THROUGH POSITIVE OUTCOMES

Identity → Values → Goals → Action Plan

↳ **Motivation** → Outcome

Webster defines motivating as "to provide with a motive." In your personal and professional life, what exactly is motivation? Why are some people more motivated than others? If you or those with whom you live and work are not highly motivated, what can be done to increase their motivation? These questions and many more have been researched by psychologists, athletes, coaches and educators for years. What is known is that people will pursue behaviors which lead to positive consequences and avoid behaviors which lead to negative consequences. Therefore, motivation is affected, in part, by the positive rewards that result from a specific action. In this chapter we will discuss how you can increase the motivation of yourself and others by increasing positive outcomes and decreasing negative ones.

In Your Personal Life

Suppose that a goal of yours is to learn how to downhill snow ski. You will persevere, even in the face of occasional "setbacks," as long as you receive positive outcomes — for example, learning how to snowplow or sidestep up a beginner's slope. Conversely, if each time you fall you become more frustrated and embarrassed (negative consequences), it is likely that you will not stick with it. The negative physical and emotional consequences you experience with each fall will, over time, cause you to avoid future skiing opportunities.

Researcher B. F. Skinner learned about this concept in an experiment with rats. If a rat pressed a lever, it was rewarded with food. And before long, the rat was a busy little lever-pusher. Skinner was known as a behaviorist, and what he discovered was a surefire way to motivate humans as well.

The best rewards are those that meet people's basic needs and wants. What do people want and need?

Some general wants and needs are:

1. Love and acceptance
2. Satisfaction from work
3. Approval of others
4. Involvement with a group
5. Feedback on job performance

These five basic needs correspond to the next four chapters in this handbook. If you want to reduce motivation to its essence, it's this:

To the degree you give others what they want,
they will give you what you want.

In Your Professional Life

Setting goals and writing action plans in and of themselves do not ensure goal achievement. You must have the personal motivation and stamina to continually apply yourself. Some experts say that by providing encouragement and incentives you can motivate someone else. Other experts say you can't motivate others — motivation comes from within.

The debate is meaningless. This book takes a much more practical approach. Its assumption is: *People don't behave in a particular way without a consequence.*

Let's say you have a choice between two activities. Whichever option gives you the most positive consequences is the one you would select.

You will be motivated to perform job-related tasks which enable you to have positive consequences such as praise or an enhanced sense of pride or visibility within the organization. Conversely, you will be demotivated to perform tasks which may lead to negative consequences such as criticism from co-workers, increased work load, conflict or even failure. Positive reinforcement is a powerful motivator. If you want to change your behavior, change the consequences.

If you are a manager or supervisor, the key to successfully motivating others is positive reinforcement; quick-fix programs or "rah-rah" speeches invariably fail. A manager or small business owner who says, "I'd give Mike more praise if he would just do a better job" has it backwards. He must give praise and recognition first (to *something* Mike does well).

There are several steps:

- Determine what the person needs.
- Present it at the appropriate time.
- Supply the reward in the appropriate way.
- Be willing to give up something to get something.

In Skinner's rat experiment, the consequence (food) was used to motivate the animal toward a particular behavior. You can also change the consequence so that someone is de-motivated from an undesirable behavior and motivated toward something more desirable. This de-motivation is known as a threat or punishment.

But negative motivation can backfire. People might seek revenge instead of making a positive change. In some circumstances, the negative attention may be perceived as being better than no attention at all and may actually cause an increase in the behavior you are trying to eliminate.

When changing behavior by changing the consequence, emphasize positive reward rather than punishment.

Success Map

Directions: Reflect on the following questions to explore motivation.

1. Do you spend more time and energy on problems or goals?
2. Who is your best friend?
3. Does your best friend help with your growth?
4. Do you spend time on your best friend's growth and life?
5. Your best friend calls you and says, *"I just wanted to call and let you know that I think you are one of the best people I know. You are smart, talented, generous, honest and make me a better person because you are my friend."* What kind of day will you have after this conversation?

Reflect on your answers. What did you learn? Do you see the impact you make on others and their impact on you?

Record three things which you can do to make an impact on someone else.

1. ______________________________
2. ______________________________
3. ______________________________

How will it also impact you?

____

____

Case Study:

You can now apply what you know about motivation to Margo.

Her needs were not being met as a computer programmer. She looked into the future and saw that the rewards were greater for her as a veterinary technician. So she decided to change. She expects to be more motivated at her new job because she'll have more contact with people and be able to work with animals.

Margo has listed her action plans for reaching the goal to become a veterinary technician within one year. Meanwhile, Margo must continue her current job as a computer programmer for several more months. As her commitment to her current job decreases, Margo finds it difficult to be motivated to do quality work. Though Margo feels badly about her decreased interest in her current job, she's not sure how to stay motivated.

Identity → Values → Goals → Action Plan

↳ **Motivation** → Outcome

In the next chapter you'll learn several additional ways to motivate yourself and others.

After reading this chapter, you will be able to:

Understand the limitations of fear, incentives and attitude as motivators;

Explain why fulfilling personal and emotional needs is the most effective motivator; and

List the eight basic personal needs which motivate.

7 MOTIVATION: FULFILLING PERSONAL AND EMOTIONAL NEEDS

Identity → Values → Goals
↓
Action Plan → **Motivation** (personal needs) → Outcome

Advertisers have successfully motivated consumers to buy their products through the use of four additional motivational methods: fear, incentives, creating a change in attitude and fulfilling personal needs. These same appeals can increase your motivation to complete your goals at both the personal and professional levels.

The most consistently proven motivational method, however, is fulfilling personal needs.

In Your Personal Life

Fear: On a personal level, fear can be a very strong motivator. If your goal is to quit smoking, the fear of disease or premature death may be an incentive to quit.

The downside of using fear to motivate yourself is that it loses its impact over time. You may learn to rationalize your actions, that is, minimize the outcome you fear so that it is no longer a motivator. For example, you might convince yourself that you will be one of the lucky ones unaffected by smoking.

Incentives: The appeal of an additional incentive or "perk" is a very strong motivator for many people. For example, that impending high school class reunion might be incentive enough to drop ten pounds!

Attitude: Telling yourself to have a "positive attitude" may or may not be an effective means of motivation. Attitudes sometimes do affect actions and feelings. Someone has said that it is easier to act your way into a new way of feeling than to feel your way into a new way of acting. The point is, a positive attitude *can* motivate you to new ways of acting and feeling. It is difficult, however, to sustain motivation solely on the basis of attitude.

Fulfilling Personal Needs: Having a goal which fulfills a personal need is a powerful incentive. Personal needs, values and beliefs are the "intangible" emotional feelings you seek to fulfill through work and family.

In Your Professional Life

Fear: Professionally, the fear of losing your job or being passed over for a promotion can be an incentive to work long hours or pursue additional education.

Using fear to motivate others, however, is usually ineffective in the long run. Recipients of threats or criticism will instinctively respond in one of two ways: fight or flight. Employee theft, excessive absenteeism, property damage and decreased productivity are all ways of fighting back. Those who choose "flight" as a response simply leave the source of their fear… their job. Rarely does fear motivate others over a long period of time.

Incentives: People who choose a career in sales are often motivated to make "just one more call" because of the possibility of earning a sale or commission incentive. However, discontinue the incentive, and motivation (and morale) will plummet. Many organizations of the '90s are experiencing budget cutbacks, resulting in the disappearance of powerful motivators: bonuses, raises, company cars and so on. The effect on productivity and employee attitude can be devastating unless the company can substitute other methods of motivating.

Attitude: Though you might motivate yourself through a positive attitude, telling others to have a positive attitude is usually an ineffective motivator. What is "positive"? What does a "positive attitude" look like? The ambiguity in this phrase leaves you powerless to change. If you are a manager or supervisor, you must remember that your role is to let employees know, in specific terms, what is expected of them, how they are currently performing and actions they can take to meet the expectations. Saying, "I want you to act positive" does not motivate because it does not tell them what to do to "act positive." In fact, they may become frustrated and experience decreased productivity or morale.

Fulfilling Personal Needs: The most consistently proven motivational method is to fulfill personal needs. The following are eight basic personal needs which motivate.

1. ***Belonging.*** Being part of a group provides us with a sense of comfort, security and partnership.
2. ***Achievement.*** To achieve gives our lives purpose, and it reinforces our self-esteem because it demonstrates our competence.
3. ***Advancement.*** To feel successful, you need to continually expand your personal and professional skills, knowledge and abilities.
4. ***Power.*** An advance in a career usually means more power or increased authority.
5. ***Responsibility.*** With responsibility comes respect, both for the person given responsibility and for the person who delegated it.
6. ***Challenge.*** Feeling challenged to grow mentally and emotionally provides a strong incentive for many people.
7. ***Recognition.*** Having others know of your achievements is essential. A letter or memo, an award, a gift or a bonus are all forms of recognition which motivate future actions.
8. ***Excellence.*** Doing an excellent job is often a reward in itself. This explains why millions of workers can find joy in their work even when it's routine.

Taking Care of Emotional Needs

Notice that almost all of these needs are personal and not financial. If higher pay and generous fringe benefits were in and of themselves enough to boost performance, the remedy for decreased productivity would be simple — increase salaries. It isn't so, because the rewards that motivate aren't solely monetary. The less tangible motivators include:

- Receiving a memo of appreciation
- Having a birthday remembered
- Being an accepted part of a group
- Having safety needs attended to
- Being listened to
- Feeling that co-workers are sensitive to personal issues

Having your emotional needs met is a far more powerful motivator than financial rewards will ever be.

Uncovering Personal Needs in Yourself and Others

By observing, asking questions and listening, you can learn which of the eight personal needs are important motivators for yourself and others. In fact, you can be an encourager and enhance the self-worth of co-workers through your words and actions.

For example, when praise or feedback is given to an employee or co-worker, the encourager makes sure it is descriptive. Rather than merely saying, "good job," the encourager says: "I was impressed at the amount of detailed information included in your report. I know you spent a lot of time working on it. Good job."

Encouragers do five important things to enhance self-worth in others:

1. Have measurable, realistic, meaningful goals
2. Allow people to participate in a task — to "own" it
3. Use training as an opportunity to stimulate excitement
4. Allow their own self-confidence to motivate others
5. Make sure goals are understood by those working to achieve them

Case Study:

Margo is now enrolled in night school. She's having trouble finding the self-discipline to work her full-time job and also study at night. She is becoming discouraged and talks to one of her instructors.

He listened to her doubts and lack of confidence about completing the program because he was a good listener. And he went a step further. He expressed his confidence in her ability to achieve her goal. He reminded Margo that her initial reasons for returning to night school were to challenge herself and advance her career. He told her of his experience whereby his diligent studies helped him diagnose a dog's illness just from a routine laboratory test he had performed — exactly the type of test Margo was having difficulty learning.

Margo was inspired to study harder because her instructor was a good listener and he appealed to Margo's personal needs of achievement and challenge.

Meeting the emotional and personal needs of yourself and others is step five on the road to success.

Identity → Values → Goals
↓
Action Plan → **Motivation** (personal needs) → Outcome

In the next chapter, we'll continue our discussion of motivation by focusing on how to give and receive both praise and reprimands.

After reading this chapter, you will be able to:

- List techniques and guidelines for giving and receiving feedback;
- Explain why the most effective feedback is positive, specific, immediate and sincere; and
- Explain why negative feedback is usually an ineffective motivator.

8 MOTIVATION THROUGH GIVING AND RECEIVING POSITIVE AND CONSTRUCTIVE FEEDBACK

Identity → Values → Goals
↓
Action Plan → **Motivation** (feedback) → Outcome

Positive and negative (constructive) feedback, when properly given and received, are powerful motivators personally and professionally.

In Your Personal Life

It has been demonstrated that pets learn more quickly if the desired behavior is reinforced immediately with praise. In the same way, positive feedback can motivate you to obtain your goals.

Throughout life your actions are evaluated by others and yourself. Self-evaluation is a way of giving and receiving feedback that helps you assess progress toward your goals. Feedback from others gives you perspective in areas that may be blindspots to you.

Though giving and receiving feedback come naturally to some, these are skills that can be learned. For example, if your friend responds defensively to your constructive feedback, you might ask yourself these questions:

- Was my comment inappropriate?
- Was our relationship such that I could offer that comment?

- Did I offer the comment sincerely and positively?

Feedback can provide motivation for personal growth if it is offered and received in a spirit of genuine concern and helpfulness.

In Your Professional Life

Feedback is not something offered only by managers and supervisors. A strong team spirit can be built when workers learn to motivate one another through positive feedback. In order for positive feedback to be effective, it must be done properly and sincerely.

Practice these techniques when giving praise.

- ***Be descriptive.*** As mentioned in the previous chapter, the more detail you can build into your positive comments, the greater the impact. Comments like "good job" or "that looks good" can be perceived as token. Take the time to tell your co-worker exactly why you think she did a good job and why her report looks good.

- ***Focus on the behavior.*** Focus your comments on the demonstrated behavior — not the personal traits. "You handled that customer's problem in a professional, timely manner" is more effective than "You were nice to that customer."

- ***Put it in writing.*** When appropriate, put your praise in writing. This can be anything from a short, handwritten note to a formal letter or memo. Putting praise in writing is long-lasting. A co-worker can reread your note, show it to family and friends or display it proudly. When you write a memo or letter of praise, don't forget to send copies to others who may have been affected by the co-worker's efforts.

- ***Make your praise timely.*** If you are a manager or supervisor, don't wait until an annual performance review to tell an employee she is doing a good job. Praise promptly when you see an employee exhibiting behavior you want to encourage. A performance review should be a time to reinforce the messages you have been giving an employee (praise and constructive criticism) all year. The "reinforcement worksheet" following the next page is especially useful for managers and supervisors.

- ***Praise regularly.*** One way to reinforce positive behavior in children is to "catch them being good." A similar approach can be used on the job. Don't wait until a co-worker does something exceptionally good to praise. Make short, descriptive praise a regular part of your interaction. For example, if you notice a co-worker has arrived early for work or is staying late to finish a project, verbalize your appreciation. If you see a co-worker making an extra effort to help a customer or a fellow employee, acknowledge it. The "positive reinforcement" worksheet on the next page will help you identify positive qualities and behaviors of your co-workers.

Success Map

Using the chart below, list 3 to 5 positive qualities or behaviors of each of your co-workers. Refer back to this list when giving positive feedback.

	Positive Qualities/Behaviors
Name:	
Name:	
Name:	

Success Map

Directions: Use the following worksheet to help you focus on reinforcement that is positive, specific, immediate, certain and sincere.

Month ____________________

Employee's Name	Date and Type of Reinforcer Used

At the end of the month, ask yourself the following:

- What changes have I observed in each employee?
- What do I need to change or continue?

Reflections

Giving and Receiving Negative or Corrective Feedback

Negative feedback is an ineffective motivator for two reasons:

- Negative reinforcement encourages employees only to meet standards; it does not encourage them to exceed standards.
- Negative reinforcement requires that the manager continually monitor performance to make sure it stays at acceptable levels. Without positive reasons for maintaining performance levels, employees easily can fall into a frame of mind that says, "When the cat's away, the mice can play."

When negative reinforcement is used routinely, it creates an unproductive work environment — the managers mistrust employees and employees learn to avoid managers and their negative influence.

Though reprimands are ineffective in producing the behavior you want, they can be effective in discouraging negative behavior.

Reprimands should:

- be used sparingly.
- specify the behavior being corrected.
- provide the employee with an alternative means of obtaining a positive reinforcer.
- be given when you are not angry.
- be given when the behavior is first exhibited.
- be given privately whenever possible.

How should you respond if you're the recipient of corrective feedback? Negative feedback can make you bitter or better. Responding defensively to corrective feedback only reinforces your supervisor's belief that the criticism is justified. Even if your supervisor fails to offer corrective feedback in constructive ways, don't forfeit the opportunity to learn from the feedback and to grow professionally.

Success Map

Directions: Complete the following grid to practice using positive reinforcement, negative reinforcement and punishment.

Situation: Describe a situation you're experiencing/ observing either personally, as a team member or as a leader.	**What type of consequence/ reinforcement has been or should be used? Why?**	**What results have you observed or should you observe?**
Situation 1		
Situation 2		
Situation 3		

Feedback: The Key to Improved Performance

Here are five guidelines for giving and receiving feedback.

- ***Solve problems***. Discuss how to avoid the same mistake again instead of berating yourself or others for what has already happened.

- ***Avoid personal attacks***. Concentrate on behavior, not personalities. Describe in detail the behavior you expect from yourself or others.

- ***Act promptly***. Deal with problems promptly once, then put them aside. Rehashing old problems will seem more like persecution than constructive criticism.

- ***Discuss problems in private***. Unlike praise, where a public display is often appropriate, criticism should be delivered in private. Whenever possible, avoid embarrassing a co-worker.

- ***Be positive***. Express confidence in yourself and others that the next time the job will be done properly.

Success Map

Directions: Circle the number representing the number of times you have done this action in the past month.

How often did you:

1. Say thank you to a co-worker for doing something they were supposed to do.

   1 2 3 4 5 6 7 8 9 10

2. Write a note/card to say "thank you" or "good job."

   1 2 3 4 5 6 7 8 9 10

3. Express confidence in someone else's ability.

   1 2 3 4 5 6 7 8 9 10

4. Acknowledge the praise given by someone else.

   1 2 3 4 5 6 7 8 9 10

5. Tell someone why they are a good co-worker/friend.

   1 2 3 4 5 6 7 8 9 10

Do you see areas in which you can improve your ability to motivate?

Success Map continued...

How well do you provide constructive feedback?

Do You:	Or	Do You:
1. Deal with the problem now.		Wait to see if it will work itself out.
2. Deal with the problem.		Tell them what you don't like.
3. Ask for their agreement.		Tell them this is the way it's to be done.
4. Take the person aside to discuss.		Blow up right then and there.
5. Tell them they'll do better next time.		Tell them if they don't shape up, they'll be shipping out.

Do you see better ways to provide feedback and bring out the best in your employees? List three things you can do to motivate and provide negative and positive feedback.

Motivating Actions	Positive and Negative Feedback
1. ______________________	1. ______________________
2. ______________________	2. ______________________
3. ______________________	3. ______________________

Reflections

Case Study:

Though her supervisor frequently finds fault with her work, Margo knows that as a computer programmer she is part of a team and others are counting on her. Even though she is no longer excited about her job, Margo enjoys the few relationships she has at work and takes pride in her performance. Margo gets little if any positive feedback from others at work, but she still feels good about the direction her life is headed in.

Margo feels much better about her studies at night school. When she recently made a mess in the lab, the instructor pulled her aside and very patiently explained how to do her exercises while cleaning up at every step. When she neatly and successfully completed her assignment, her instructor told her exactly why he was proud of her work.

Effective motivators go out of their way to give praise. It makes them feel good, and they know it does the same for others. Motivators also don't avoid handing out constructive feedback, but they do so sparingly and with care.

Identity → Values → Goals
↓
Action Plan → **Motivation** (feedback) → Outcome

In the next chapter, we'll discuss how workers are motivated through involvement in the organization.

After reading this chapter, you will be able to:

Explain why participatory management is the style of management for the '90s;

Name five benefits of participatory management; and

Determine the level of involvement in your business or organization after completing the "Involvement" Success Map.

9 USING INVOLVEMENT TO MOTIVATE

Identity → Values → Goals
↓
Action Plan → **Motivation** (involvement) → Outcome

Informed involvement in planning, implementing goals and solving problems is an effective means to motivate yourself and others.

In Your Personal Life

In an earlier chapter, you learned that effective goal-setting depends on a clear sense of personal identity and values. Your identity and values will determine the goals which you work toward. No goal, however, is obtainable without personal involvement and commitment. You will be motivated to reach your goals only to the extent that you have made these goals your own. Motivation springs from active involvement. Recall that in our case study Margo was motivated to make significant changes in her personal and professional life. These changes required planning, goal-setting and commitment to a course of action. Change is rarely accomplished in life without personal involvement and dedication. When the commitment is high, however, the motivation to change is strong.

In Your Professional Life

The changing shape of management

Involvement in an organization is no longer a one-way street.

In the past, "top down" management was the rule. Workers were told to follow orders. Their input was rarely solicited, but...

- Who knows most about the problems in the workplace?
- Who has greater knowledge of customers' needs?
- Who knows more about safety needs?

Answer: the workers. People doing the work know more about the company's problems and needs than anyone else.

Frontline employees' opinions are being solicited more and more because...

- Attitudes toward authority are changing. Workers are demanding to be heard.
- Workers expect to participate in planning. They're better educated and have good ideas they expect will be listened to.

Contemporary management is now asking all levels of the organization to become involved in these functions:

- Helping determine a company's mission and objectives
- Analyzing organizational structure
- Formulating long-range goals
- Organizing meaningful jobs related to the company's mission

Success Map

Directions: Answer the following questions by circling true or false. These questions will indicate whether you feel "involved" in your business or organization.

1.	I know the #1 goal for my company.	T	F
2.	I know the #1 goal for my department/division.	T	F
3.	I know how my role impacts the company.	T	F
4.	I give input to the goals for the department/division.	T	F
5.	I am rewarded for good ideas which save the company money.	T	F
6.	I know the company's profit/loss this quarter.	T	F
7.	I am comfortable in bringing problems to the table.	T	F
8.	I know the break-even point for the company.	T	F
9.	I promote the company through contact with clients.	T	F
10.	I am told why a change is taking place.	T	F

Are you informed and involved? Did you think you were informed before you answered the above questions? After answering the questions, do you still think you're informed? Circle the statements you're not sure about.

Work groups can contribute to decision-making and planning. Participatory management means seeking employees' opinions whenever possible and keeping an open mind to the suggestions and criticisms they offer.

Benefits of Participatory Management

1. ***It's a powerful motivator.*** When you feel you are part of a team and have a significant influence on decisions, you are more likely to accept the decisions and seek solutions to difficult problems. In short, you own what you do and where you work.

2. ***Better decisions result.*** The more facts you have available when making a decision, the better equipped you are to make a sound one. This is sometimes called the synergy effect.

3. ***A trusting climate is created.*** An environment of trust develops when people have respect for each other's judgment. It is important for workers to know not only what is being done but *why*. Honesty, openness, consistency and respect are vital components of trust.

4. ***Employees understand their jobs better.*** If you are a manager or small business owner, ask your employees to write descriptions of their jobs, including specific responsibilities. Also ask them to prepare at least three job objectives.

5. ***Progress toward goals is accelerated.*** Once objectives are established, managers and employees should have frequent discussions about how the work is progressing. Good listening should be practiced, and all opinions should be respected and heard.

Participatory management should be practiced all the time, not sporadically. Some organizations have found that formal suggestion programs are helpful.

Employee involvement, in many aspects of an organization's operations, is the new reality of the 1990s. Group problem-solving and planning almost always produce results far superior to a more centralized form of management.

Success Map

Trust is critical to the success of an organization.

As an employee are you encouraged to be:

• Honest	1	2	3	4	5
	Seldom				Frequently
• Open	1	2	3	4	5
	Seldom				Frequently
• Consistent	1	2	3	4	5
	Seldom				Frequently
• Respectful	1	2	3	4	5
	Seldom				Frequently

What is one thing you can do to improve the trust quotient?

____

____

____

What is the most important thing you'd like your manager to do to improve trust within the organization?

____

____

____

Case Study:

Margo is now a proud graduate of night school.

Just a few weeks after Margo started her new job, the owner of the clinic received the financial statements for the previous fiscal year. The clinic was losing money.

All the employees, including Margo, got together to figure out how to stop the flow of red ink. As the discussion progressed, she realized that it wasn't the quantity of business that was the problem, but rather the billing system.

Margo drew on her past experience to suggest that a computer be used to standardize rates and produce invoices immediately after a patient visit. If payment doesn't arrive within 30 days, the computer signals that the account needs attention.

Everyone acknowledged that billing was a problem and that computerizing the system was the likely solution. Margo couldn't remember the last time her self-esteem had been so high.

Using involvement to motivate is a necessary part of step five on your road map to success.

People are motivated when they can see clearly and concretely how they are doing.

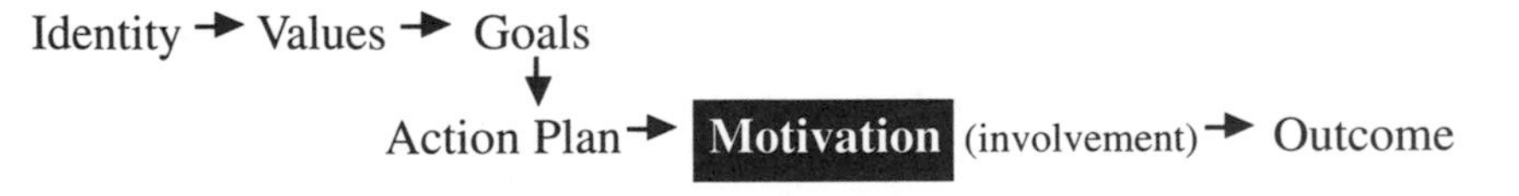

We'll continue our discussion of motivation in chapter 10, when we'll focus on the concept of keeping score.

After reading this chapter, you will be able to:

- Explain why keeping score is great motivator;
- List four guidelines for keeping score; and
- Set up a performance feedback system to measure progress toward your goals.

10 MOTIVATION: KEEPING SCORE

Identity → Values → Goals
↓
Action Plan → **Motivation** (keeping score) → Outcome

In Your Personal Life

Keeping score is a great motivator and is essential for success. When you know how you're doing, you naturally want to do better.

Although personal success can't always be quantified, measurable results usually are powerful motivators. Professional sports teams have developed sophisticated techniques for charting player performance. Students measure progress by grades, dieters by pounds and body builders by inches. "Success breeds success," especially when it is measured, posted and celebrated.

Based on what you have learned so far, keeping score is an integral part of achieving personal success. You should:

- Determine your values
- Set measurable goals
- Develop action plans
- Chart your progress
- Celebrate your accomplishments

In Your Professional Life

Businesses and organizations also keep score. Here are some examples of key performance areas that can be measured:

- Output/productivity
- Profitability
- Financial measures commonly found on balance sheets
- Employee and customer attitudes
- Market share
- Sales quotas

Guidelines for "Keeping Score"

1. ***Gain as much information as you can.*** You can learn how you're contributing to the final score through feedback on your regular job performance.

2. ***The most useful information is measurable.*** If you are a manager, measure and post only those behaviors or actions you and your employees can see and improve upon: attendance, quotas, quality control, etc. The "Keeping Score" worksheet is especially helpful for managers or supervisors.

3. ***Establish a baseline.*** Calculate your average performance over a period of several weeks, then calculate future performance as measured against the average. Also post a goal. People love to see the line on that graph go up with time.

Sample graph:

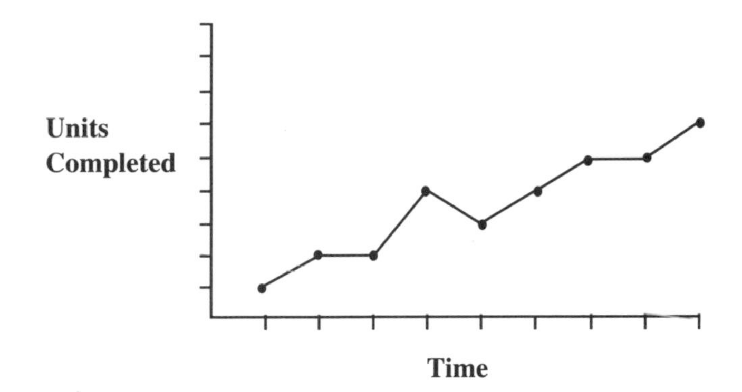

4. ***Post performance figures often.*** Too many organizations or businesses wait until quarterly or yearly reports come out before reports are posted. Then these tools have lost much of their motivational value. Post figures as soon as they are available.

There are two main benefits of keeping score. First, it shows you are paying attention to goals, action plans and people. Second, keeping score is fun. It brings people together as part of a team.

Keeping score can be a two-way street. You do not have to wait for your employer to chart your progress. You can do this yourself. Follow the guidelines found in the "Designing Feedback Systems" worksheet to learn how to set up a feedback system to measure your own progress toward your professional goals. Don't forget to celebrate your accomplishments!

Success Map

Directions: List below five things you feel would improve performance and motivate employees.

1. ______________________________
2. ______________________________
3. ______________________________
4. ______________________________
5. ______________________________

How will you measure these five things?

1. ______________________________
2. ______________________________
3. ______________________________
4. ______________________________
5. ______________________________

List below the baseline or where you are now for these five things. (If you don't know, how will you find the baseline?)

1. ______________________________
2. ______________________________
3. ______________________________
4. ______________________________
5. ______________________________

List below the goal and improvement (where you want to be) for each of these five things, e.g., cost, improved efficiency.

1. ______________________________
2. ______________________________
3. ______________________________
4. ______________________________
5. ______________________________

You now have all the information needed to chart where you are and where you're going. Make charts from these and post in a place where all can see. Watch for results!

Reflections

Success Map

Performance-feedback systems need to focus on improvement. Feedback is information on past performance (or behavior). Feedback is specific so employees know exactly what to do to change or improve.

Feedback systems should be:

- Visual
- Graphically easy to understand
- A graph with a title or slogan
- A graph showing a baseline
- A graph showing improvements
- A graph showing positive information
- A graph relating to things only the employees can do
- Bottom-line results oriented

Remember, the employee/performer needs to have the knowledge and skills to improve performance, or the feedback system will de-motivate and not produce improvements.

Case Study:

Margo thought she was doing a good job, but she wasn't sure. She brought up her concern at a meeting, and the discussion that followed generated a new system of keeping score.

They decided that at the end of each week two graphs would be posted reflecting the output of that week. One would measure the number of patients treated each day, another would measure average waiting time for the patients. They learned that the clinic was treating an average of 15 patients each day, with an average waiting time of 20 minutes. The next month's goal was set at 18 patients a day, with an average waiting time of 15 minutes. Here is how the graphs looked:

Number of Patients

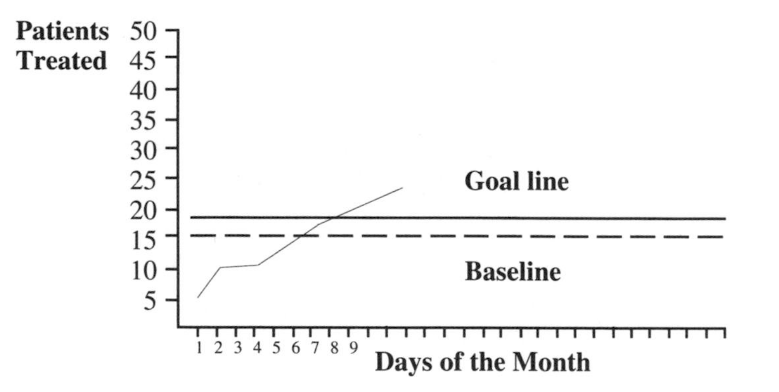

How Long Do Our Patients Wait?

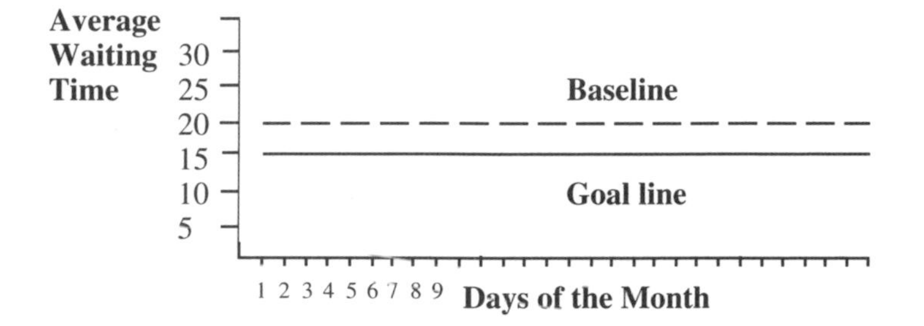

Margo began to experiment with a new way to use exam rooms so that they were in use more often. The graph started to show improvement in the second week.

At the end of the month when their goals were reached, the owner of the clinic threw a surprise celebration party. Margo was already part of a team; now she felt as if she were part of a "second family."

Keeping score is an important ingredient in motivating people.

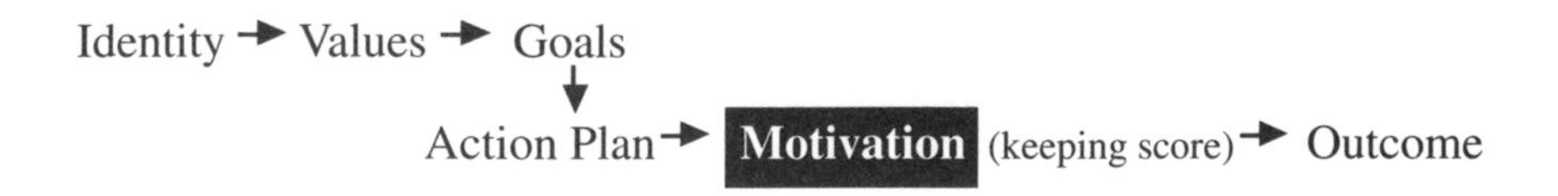

Throughout the discussion on motivation, an underlying theme has been the need for self-motivation. In the next chapter, we will give special attention to this important ingredient of motivation.

After reading this chapter, you will be able to:

List four guidelines for achieving self-motivation in your personal life;

List four guidelines for achieving self-motivation in your professional life; and

Start developing self-motivation by completing the "Contract for Success."

11 SELF-MOTIVATION

Identity → Values → Goals
↓
Action Plan → **Motivation** (self) → Outcome

Motivation is the inner desire that keeps you always moving forward in spite of discouragement, mistakes and setbacks.

Motivation is not something that comes naturally for everyone. It can be learned and developed. How do you build this inner desire?

In Your Personal Life

1. ***Believe in yourself.*** Allow only positive thoughts to dominate your thinking, such as:

    - I am worthy.
    - I like myself.
    - I am strong and self-secure.
    - I can handle what comes my way.
    - I know the future holds opportunities for me.

Forcing yourself to think this way may be difficult at first. Only when you believe that you deserve success can it possibly come your way.

2. ***Overcome fear.*** Fear creates stress, panic and anxiety. Fear defeats your plans and goals. Here are some ways you can overcome fear:

    - Build self-confidence.

    - Identify and understand your fears.

    - Take action. Once you start to do something, your fears will disappear.

3. ***Build on failures and mistakes.*** Socrates once remarked that there is more risk in buying knowledge than food. He is correct. If you purchase spoiled meat, you throw it out, not allowing it to harm your body. But ideas imprinted on the mind are not so easily dislodged. Once you learn from your failures and mistakes, they should be discarded like spoiled food. To judge yourself only in light of your failures and mistakes is to assure more of the same.

4. ***Start now.*** Get in motion as soon as possible, and as your momentum builds, so will your motivation.

In Your Professional Life

1. ***Welcome challenges.*** Challenges are opportunities to break out of the routine of your job and expand your skills. Challenges can be springboards to professional growth if they are welcomed as opportunities rather than tolerated as nuisances. You are more likely to be motivated to a higher level of job performance if you embrace positively the challenges that come your way.

2. ***Take pride in achievements.*** In the last chapter you learned that keeping score can provide a tangible way to measure progress. As progress is made, it is important to take pride in your achievements. Though you cannot overlook the problems of tomorrow, you should not forget to celebrate the successes of today. Even small achievements can be occasions for pride.

3. ***Visualize success.*** As clearly and vividly as you can, you should visualize the rewards of your success in your mind. Make it such a good picture that you'll do almost anything to be part of it.

4. ***Be flexible.*** Sometimes self-motivation is lacking because of failure to adapt or change. It is possible to hold a goal too tightly. For example, failure to reach unrealistic goals can cause your self-image to plummet. The solution to the problem may be flexibility — a willingness to adapt goals so they more nearly fit your values and skills. In chapter 13 we will have more to say about flexibility.

Case Study:

Margo decided to alter her career, life-style and financial situation. These changes have caused her doubt and worry.

Here are the steps she took to develop self-motivation.

1. *She made a written contract with herself* to increase her sense of self-worth. Her contract states:

    - I have the intelligence to succeed in whatever I try.
    - I am building new relationships.
    - I am in control of my finances.
    - I have the discipline to comply with this contract.

2. *She formed clear mental images* that allow her to see herself in a new way. She visualized herself as having a warm feeling of inner satisfaction for achieving her goals.

3. *She identified and confronted her fears.* With risk comes the possibility of failure. It can't be avoided, Margo told herself, and so she has confronted one more obstacle in her journey toward success.

4. *She built on past failures and mistakes* by learning from and not being victimized by them.

5. *She began a time-management system.* Each day she filled out a personal time budget. It forced her to start now on those things necessary to accomplish her goals.

6. *She remained flexible* when her plans did not always go according to schedule.

7. *She focused on the rewards waiting for her* at the end of her journey, including working with animals, having a better circle of friends and achieving financial responsibility.

Make the commitment to work hard for your own personal reasons. Start now, and self-motivation will begin to build within you. Take a minute to complete your contract for success.

Identity → Values → Goals
↓
Action Plan → **Motivation** (self) → Outcome

I, ____________________, do hereby state that I will focus on the following five positive reinforcers:

- ____
- ____
- ____
- ____
- ____

I have identified my strengths and weaknesses. I will not waste time by focusing on the following energy wasters:

- ____
- ____
- ____
- ____
- ____

This prepares me to be successful in (list five things you want to achieve):

- ____
- ____
- ____
- ____
- ____

This contract is a binding contract for a successful life.

______________________________ ______________

Signature Date

Place this contract where it will serve as a periodic reminder of where you are, where you're going and how you're going to get there.

After reading this chapter, you will be able to:

- List four guidelines for achieving discipline in your personal life;
- List four guidelines for achieving discipline on the job; and
- Identify one area personally and professionally where you need more self-discipline.

12 SELF-DISCIPLINE: KEEPING YOURSELF ON THE ROAD TO SUCCESS

Identity → Values → Goals → Action Plan
↓
Motivation → **Discipline** → Outcome

Self-discipline is hard work. People who get the job done, even when the job is unpleasant, have developed a mental toughness that comes from practice, patience and the ability to see beyond the immediate task.

In Your Personal Life

Self-discipline involves doing what *needs* to be done rather than what you would *like* to do. Here are some guidelines.

1. ***Take responsibility for yourself.*** You are responsible for managing your own life. You alone have the power to fulfill those goals you have set for yourself. Take responsibility for meeting those goals by taking action.

2. ***Review your priorities.*** Even highly disciplined persons find it easy to get off track. If you don't know where you're going, it doesn't matter what route you take or when you get there. Periodic review of your priorities will keep you focused.

3. ***Start small.*** If many areas of your life seem chaotic or unmanageable, then start working on one area and ignore the others for now.

   Jerry wanted to begin exercising regularly. Some of his friends had disciplined regimens before or after work. Jerry, however, left for work tired and returned home in the evenings tired. Jerry needs to start small. Perhaps the discipline of a health club one night a week might help. Or Jerry could spend fifteen minutes of his lunch break on a vigorous walk or take the stairs rather than the elevator.

   The key is to get started! Once you start, you'll develop momentum, and the task won't seem so hard.

4. ***Reward yourself.*** Discipline should not be drudgery. After tackling an especially difficult task, reward yourself. Even an anticipated brief break from an unpleasant chore can provide the proverbial carrot on the stick to press on.

Discipline on the Job

Here are guidelines for self-discipline to make your organization or business successful.

1. ***Set an example.*** Business owners and managers cannot expect their employees to practice self-discipline if they don't set an example. Moreover, disciplined employees inspire one another to be their best.

2. ***Focus on specific goals.*** The key to self-discipline is being able to defer your gratification from the present to the future. The best gratification comes when you realize your goals.

3. ***Identify time-wasters.*** Some examples of time-wasters include not organizing your telephone time (when you return calls, when you make calls), giving in to distractions (visitors, getting coffee, etc.) and attending poorly organized, unproductive meetings. Also, look for ways to reduce paperwork.

4. ***Work smart.*** Some strategies for working smart include:

    - planning ahead
    - organizing projects into manageable segments
    - scheduling demanding work at peak performance times

Case Study:

Margo is now several months into her new job as a veterinary technician, and the initial excitement is starting to wear off. Her goal is to be appointed the head tech, and she knows she must practice good work habits to earn that promotion. Yet sometimes she finds herself cutting corners on certain procedures.

To make matters worse, her financial situation is still tight. She knows she should be doing better.

Margo decides to change her habits. She reviews her priorities and reminds herself of her long-range goals. She does this each time she is tempted to cut corners or spend money unnecessarily. Within a few weeks, she doesn't even think about cutting corners.

Margo also forces herself to avoid the shopping center on the way home. She begins following the budget she had previously outlined for herself, and at the end of the month she is able to pay all her bills when they are due. Margo is learning discipline.

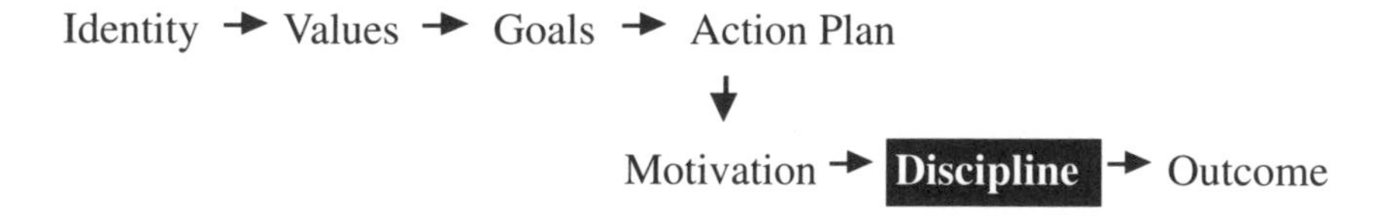

Exercising self-discipline is the key to achieving your personal and professional goals. In the next chapter, we'll discuss the role flexibility plays in your journey to success.

Success Map

Sometimes discipline is easier if it is structured around a system. Try one of the following systems to achieve your goals and master improvements.

1. Purchase a notebook and incorporate the exercise sheets from this book; organize with tabs/dividers in the notebook. You will need a section for the following things:

    - Calendar
    - To Do Lists (one for personal, one for professional)
    - Ideas and Goals
    - Wish List
    - Phone Numbers/Addresses

2. Another option is a programmed time-management system, e.g., calendar, daily to dos. Personalize this system too, by adding your personal affirmation statements, goals and visual reminders. This system will serve as a motivator to keep you on track, on time and focused on success daily.

3. Computer software is now available to help with time management. If computer work is part of your daily routine, this might be an important aid to discipline. However, be careful. It is also easy to waste time on computers.

After reading this chapter, you will be able to:

Describe how change can be a positive force in your personal life;

Assess your openness to change; and

List five steps for coping with change on the job.

13 FLEXIBILITY: HOW TO RESPOND TO CHANGE

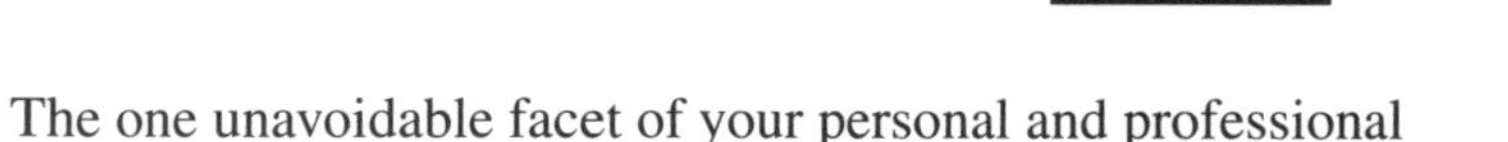

The one unavoidable facet of your personal and professional life is change.

Here are three key aspects of change.

1. Change is constant and unavoidable.

2. Change creates fear.

3. People tend to resist change.

Change is frightening because it threatens your sense of security. Your survival and that of your organization or business is directly related to your ability to adapt to change.

There are basically two ways to react to change. If you are a type D, you have danger-oriented reaction to change. You avoid change, fear it and attack it. If you are type O, you view change as an opportunity. You accept it and acknowledge its uncertainty.

Review the chart below and complete the self-assessment:

Outcomes: Type O, Type D

Type O	**Type D**
Accepts change Acknowledges uncertainty	Avoids change Blames, attacks, protects self from counterattacks
Positions change as a problem to solve, not a dilemma to avoid	Immobilized by fear Lower level of creativity and problem solving
Outcome Problem solving/recycle	***Outcome*** No action/dead end

Self-Assessment

What characteristics/traits do you have that are:

Type O	**Type D**
______________________	______________________
______________________	______________________
______________________	______________________
______________________	______________________

My strongest trait is: ______________________________

A trait I would like to modify or change is: ____________________

Change in Your Personal Life

Change can become a positive force in your life if you learn coping techniques. Here are some healthy ways to view and adapt to change.

1. ***See change as an opportunity, not as a problem.*** Change is growth, and despite the anxiety it causes, it can significantly improve your life if you let it.

2. ***Don't just stand there, change.*** You make the choice: Do nothing and let change happen to you, or look for the opportunities and make it work for you.

3. ***Accept change in your life as normal and positive.*** Re-evaluate your goals daily. Don't be so rigid and fearful of change that you pursue a goal that, when reached, holds no reward for you.

Change on the Job

Experiencing change in your workplace can be somewhat unsettling. There are a huge number of jobs or business variables that can change — some of which you have control over, some of which you don't:

- A transfer
- A new boss
- New competition
- New markets
- New technology

Five Steps to Coping with Change

1. ***Re-evaluate values, goals and action plans.*** Be sensitive to subtle changes that may indicate more profound future changes. Is your product or service about to be regulated? Will the changing social or economic forces affect your business? These are important issues to be aware of even if you don't own the company.

2. ***Use knowledge to kill fear.*** Head off fear, rumors and trouble in advance. Communicate change *before* it happens by learning:

    - What the change will be
    - Where it will occur
    - Who will be affected and in what way
    - Why it is being made
    - When it will go into effect
    - How it will be implemented

3. ***Accentuate the positive.*** Focus on the new opportunities that are available. The more positive you are, the more co-workers will approach change the same way.

4. ***Be patient.*** It takes time for old habits to die and new ones to be born. Though changes can occur practically overnight, you need time to assimilate change.

5. ***Provide reassurance.*** People often define their identities by their jobs. Let them know you still value and respect them. Their self-esteem will remain intact, and change will be accepted more readily.

Case Study:

Margo has worked for the animal clinic for one year. Yet things have been far from stable. Three major changes have tested Margo's resilience.

First, because of her background in computer programming, Margo was used to fill in for two months for the billing clerk, who went on maternity leave.

Second, changing technology makes it impossible to learn all in school that a veterinary technician needs to know. Margo has already had to do some additional evening study to keep her skills current.

Third, the veterinarian with whom Margo worked opened his own office in another city. Margo has had to learn to work with a new veterinarian who does things differently from her previous boss.

In all three changes Margo has responded with flexibility. Why?

- She knew these changes were beyond her control.
- She believed she would be challenged to grow.
- She confronted her fear of change by gaining knowledge. For example, she knew her work as billing clerk was temporary and would contribute to the total effectiveness of the business.

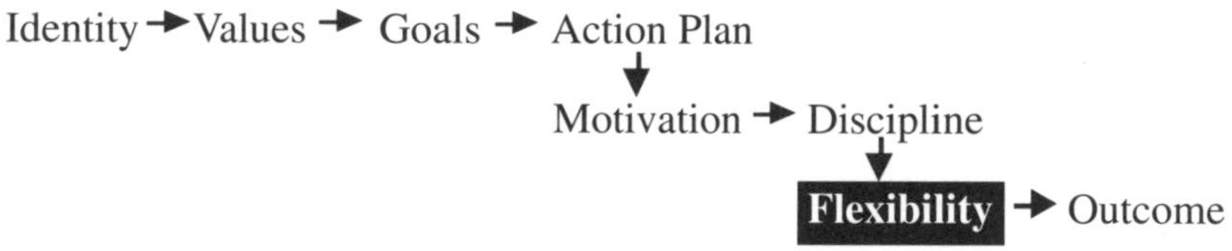

Identity → Values → Goals → Action Plan
↓
Motivation → Discipline
↓
Flexibility → Outcome

Flexibility — that ability to roll with the punches — will keep you on the road to success. In the final chapter, we'll discuss your ultimate destination.

Success Map

Directions: Cope with change by controlling or at least influencing events. Take charge by determining…

- What is it that I want or desire as a result of the change?

- Why do I want this result?

- What resources are available to help me achieve what I want?

- What is my plan?

- When will I take the first step in my plan?

After reading this chapter, you will be able to:

- Explain how a goal differs from an outcome;
- Understand the importance of identity, values, goals, action plans, motivation and discipline to your outcomes; and
- Identify several principles to follow in order to achieve your outcomes.

14 THE OUTCOME OF YOUR JOURNEY

Identity → Values → Goals → Action Plan
↓
Motivation → Discipline
↓
Flexibility → **Outcome**

Outcomes are both similar to and different from goals. Goals are specific, defined objectives with ways to measure your progress in a given timeframe. Your outcome is what actually happens, which may or may not be what you originally targeted on your success map. Sometimes the outcome is better than your original objective!

In Your Personal Life

As you seek to achieve your desired outcome, keep the following principles in mind.

1. ***Your outcome should be consistent with your identity and values.*** From time to time, review the worksheets in chapters 2 and 3. This will help you seek outcomes which are consistent with who you would like to become.

2. ***Your actions should support your desired outcome.*** If you have a clear understanding of your ultimate destination, then your actions can be evaluated in light of your outcomes. Give time and energy to activities that promote your aims. If your ultimate aim is to earn a college degree, set goals and determine action plans that will support that aim.

3. ***Sustain motivation to reach your outcome.*** Review the worksheets in chapters 6 to 11 to recall different techniques for motivation. Without proper motivation, the eight-step success model breaks down. Goals, action plans and outcomes are useless without proper motivation.

4. ***Stay disciplined.*** Discipline is the ability to see beyond the immediate task to the ultimate outcome. You can accomplish tasks in your personal life, even unpleasant ones, if you keep envisioning your outcome.

In Your Professional Life

When you evaluate the results of your professional journey, keep these things in mind.

1. ***Hold your outcome in high regard.*** Even if you fell short of your initial goals, you gained valuable experience along the way. Cherish your past because it is your springboard to the future.

2. ***Take pride in your successes.*** If you accomplish your objective, take great pride in your achievement. Revel in it, but don't stop. There are other exciting goals for you to achieve. If you didn't quite reach your objective, look at it this way:

    - At least you tried.

    - All successful people fail. Do what they do: Give yourself permission to fail. You have learned great lessons. You are now better equipped for success.

    - Don't dwell on it. Forgive yourself.

- Don't place blame. No one else is responsible for your failure. Blaming keeps you stuck in one place.

3. ***Focus on what you did right, not what you did wrong.*** Successful people work smarter, not harder. Determine what specific skills produced your best results and develop them.

4. ***If this handbook doesn't work for you the first time, try again.*** Habits take practice and perseverance. Don't give up.

5. ***Set another outcome.*** Now that you've arrived at your outcome, it's time to set another objective. Schedule a period of rest after reaching your first outcome, then start on the journey again.

Achieving success is a constant process, never a destination in itself. You should always keep trying to improve and strive for excellence.

Life is growth. Your successes are to be savored, but it's the journey that provides the most excitement and fun. *See you on the road!*

Index

Notes

Notes

Notes

Buy any 3, get 1 FREE!

BUY 3 GET 1 FREE! Buy more, save more!

Get a 60-Minute Training Series™ Handbook FREE ($14.95 value)* when you buy any three. See back of order form for full selection of titles.

These are helpful how-to books for you, your employees and co-workers. Add to your library. Use for new-employee training, brown-bag seminars, promotion gifts and more. Choose from many popular titles on a variety of lifestyle, communication, productivity and leadership topics exclusively from National Press Publications.

DESKTOP HANDBOOK ORDER FORM

Ordering is easy:

1. Complete both sides of this Order Form, detach, and mail, fax or phone your order to:

Mail: National Press Publications
P.O. Box 419107
Kansas City, MO 64141-6107

Fax: 1-913-432-0824
Phone: 1-800-258-7248
Internet: www.NationalSeminarsTraining.com

2. Please print:

Name______________________ Position/Title ______________________
Company/Organization____
Address______________________ City ______________________
State/Province______________________ ZIP/Postal Code ______________________
Telephone (____)______________________ Fax (____) ______________________
Your e-mail: ____

3. Easy payment:

❑ Enclosed is my check or money order for $__________ (total from back).
Please make payable to National Press Publications.

Please charge to:
❑ MasterCard ❑ VISA ❑ American Express

Credit Card No. ______________________ Exp. Date______________________
Signature____

MORE WAYS TO SAVE:

SAVE 33%!!! BUY 20-50 COPIES of any title ... pay just $9.95 each ($13.25 Canadian).

SAVE 40%!!! BUY 51 COPIES OR MORE of any title ... pay just $8.95 each ($11.95 Canadian).

* $20.00 in Canada

VIP No. 922-008438-099

Buy 3, get 1 FREE!

60-MINUTE TRAINING SERIES™ HANDBOOKS

TITLE	ITEM #	RETAIL PRICE*	QTY	TOTAL
8 Steps for Highly Effective Negotiations	#424	$14.95		
Assertiveness	#4422	$14.95		
Balancing Career and Family	#4152	$14.95		
Common Ground	#4122	$14.95		
Delegate for Results	#4592	$14.95		
The Essentials of Business Writing	#4310	$14.95		
Everyday Parenting Solutions	#4862	$14.95		
Exceptional Customer Service	#4882	$14.95		
Fear & Anger: Slay the Dragons ...	#4302	$14.95		
Fundamentals of Planning	#4301	$14.95		
Getting Things Done	#4112	$14.95		
How to Coach an Effective Team	#4308	$14.95		
How to De-Junk Your Life	#4306	$14.95		
How to Handle Conflict and Confrontation	#4952	$14.95		
How to Manage Your Boss	#493	$14.95		
How to Supervise People	#4102	$14.95		
How to Work With People	#4032	$14.95		
Inspire & Motivate: Performance Reviews	#4232	$14.95		
Listen Up: Hear What's Really Being Said	#4172	$14.95		
Motivation and Goal-Setting	#4962	$14.95		
A New Attitude	#4432	$14.95		
The New Dynamic Comm. Skills for Women	#4309	$14.95		
The Polished Professional	#4262	$14.95		
The Power of Innovative Thinking	#428	$14.95		
The Power of Self-Managed Teams	#4222	$14.95		
Powerful Communication Skills	#4132	$14.95		
Present With Confidence	#4612	$14.95		
The Secret to Developing Peak Performers	#4692	$14.95		
Self-Esteem: The Power to Be Your Best	#4642	$14.95		
Shortcuts to Organized Files & Records	#4307	$14.95		
The Stress Management Handbook	#4842	$14.95		
Supreme Teams: How to Make Teams Work	#4303	$14.95		
Thriving on Change	#4212	$14.95		
Women and Leadership	#4632	$14.95		

Sales Tax

All purchases subject to state and local sales tax.

Questions?

Call

1-800-258-7248

Subtotal	$
Add 7% Sales Tax *(Or add appropriate state and local tax)*	$
Shipping and Handling** *($6 one item; 50¢ each additional item)*	$
TOTAL	$

**Free Freight on all orders over $150.00

* $20.00 in Canada

Motivation & Goal-Setting

The Keys to Achieving Success

Written by Jim Cairo

Edited by National Press Publications

NATIONAL PRESS PUBLICATIONS

A Division of Rockhurst College Continuing Education Center, Inc.

6901 West 63rd Street • P.O. Box 2949 • Shawnee Mission, Kansas 66201-1349

1-800-258-7248 • 1-913-432-7757

Motivation & Goal-Setting: The Keys to Achieving Success

Published by National Press Publications

Printed in the United States of America

20

ISBN 1-55852-155-0